St. Joseph Church
St. Francis Group
Room 107

This Side of Resurrection

Meditations on the Way of the Cross for Our Daily Lives

BY MARY JO TULLY

Our Sunday Visitor Publishing Division
Our Sunday Visitor, Inc.
Huntington, Indiana 46750

For the person who reads my unpublished thoughts . . .

◊ ◊ ◊

This work originally appeared in the March - October 1988 issues of *Emmanuel* magazine, published by the Congregation of the Blessed Sacrament and the Priests' Eucharistic League, and reprinted by permission of said publisher. Scripture excerpts in this work are taken from the *New American Bible With Revised New Testament*, ©1986 by the Confraternity of Christian Doctrine, Washington, D.C.. All rights reserved.
Copyright © 1989 by Our Sunday Visitor Publishing Division
Our Sunday Visitor, Inc.

ALL RIGHTS RESERVED

With the exception of short excerpts for critical reviews, no part of this book may be reproduced or transmitted in any form or by any means, electronic or mechanical, including photocopying, recording, or by any information storage or retrieval system, without permission in writing from the publisher.
Write:
Our Sunday Visitor Publishing Division
Our Sunday Visitor, Inc.
200 Noll Plaza
Huntington, Indiana 46750

ISBN: 0-87973-361-6

PRINTED IN THE UNITED STATES OF AMERICA

Cover design by Clete Olinger

Preface

Like many adults, I remember the Stations of the Cross as part of my experience in a Catholic school. Each Friday during Lent, we moved from station to station as the priest reflected on the suffering of Jesus. As a child, I was remembering how the Lord gave himself for me. As a child, I left those stations behind me on Easter Sunday. As an adult, my participation changed little — except it was voluntary. I still associated the Stations of the Cross with a physical movement through the church and a focusing on the passion of the Lord. And I still left them behind on Easter Sunday.

As I grew older, the devotion became more a remembrance than a reality. The Eucharist became central to my Christian existence, though memories of the passion garnered from the experience added richness to the Eucharistic Prayer and to the meaning of the liturgy. It was not until I was asked to do a Lenten retreat for a group of priests that I seriously thought about what those stations might mean for the life of a Christian if they were not simply relegated to a specific time and a place. Even I was surprised when I uncovered the richness of the devotion, when I learned adulthood and maturity are the most creative Christian environment for discovering the Stations as a way of life.

The Stations of the Cross ought not be hidden in a nostalgic corner of the prayer life of the Christian or the liturgy of the Church. The deepest meaning of the devotion is ingrained in our life though we seldom pause to reflect upon it. We live these stations every day.

Though this book is essentially meant for personal meditation, there are some who will find it helpful to discuss the thoughts presented here — to disagree with them and to enrich them. For this reason, it might be helpful to use it as source material for parish discussion and prayer groups. Hopefully, this would never be done without prayerful thought focusing on the individual's own relationship with the suffering Jesus and community prior to what might otherwise be merely a purely intellectual exercise.

Mary Jo Tully

THE FIRST STATION
Jesus Is Condemned to Death

(courtesy of John Zierten)

"Again the high priest asked him and said to him, 'Are you the Messiah, the son of the Blessed One?' Then Jesus answered, 'I am...' At that the high priest tore his garments and said, 'What further need have we of witnesses? You have heard the blasphemy. What do you think?' They all condemned him as deserving to die."
(Mark 14:61-64)

We don't call it "condemnation" today. We have other names for subjecting one another to the alienation and pain that comes from that verdict. Some never hear the sentence pronounced but feel its implications throughout entire lifetimes. Again and again, they ask themselves: "What did I do to deserve this?" In fact, many have done nothing. Still, their very condemnation leads them to a journey filled with "free-floating guilt." They suffer the anxiety of having offended without being able to specify the offense. None of us is totally free of either the condemnation or the guilt. It is important to remember the Lord has not condemned us. He has, instead, set us free. Our condemnation — and our guilt — comes from a community not always sensitive to the pain it inflicts on its members.

We have — all of us — not only been condemned ourselves but have participated in the condemnation of many others. Sophisticated and subtle as we are, the condemnation has sometimes been a mere smirk. On other occasions, it has been whispered in confidential tones across a luncheon table "just between us girls," at cocktail parties, and even in board rooms.

More blatantly, we have — sometimes with neither malice nor forethought — participated in the condemnation of total communities by either our lack of action on behalf of the poor and impoverished or through our willingness to be silent when injustice in both our country and our Church has caused suffering to the victims of our silence.

One of the symptoms of this wholesale condemnation of life can be seen in the continually rising rate of suicide in our country. There are those who would look to those who have taken their lives for an explanation when — perhaps — we ought to more seriously examine the attitudes of modern society toward life.

Is it really unusual that young people today wonder what life is about and how much it is worth? Abortion and euthanasia fill the pages of our daily newspaper. Ghetto murders in our large cities are not even considered newsworthy. Violence is a way of survival for many. One of the most serious questions the human community might ask itself is whether or not the problem of suicide among the very young is more their attitude or the attitude of modern society.

Condemned to death . . . it's not a new sentence. But in our own stations of the cross, there is an underlying echo that we dare not forget. Just as Jesus heard resurrection in every step along the way, we hear life in every word of death and joy in every sorrow. We hear it first as a community in the very story of creation.

"By the sweat of your face shall you get bread to eat, until you return to the ground, from which you were taken. For you are dirt and to dirt you shall return." (Genesis 3:19)

No matter how positive our personal attitude toward life, we have not escaped a basic "condemnation to death" and the symptoms that come from it. Wrested from the safe wombs of our mothers, we cried — most of us loudly and lustily. We cried for many reasons: because we had left the safety of our mothers; but, also because we realized that once thrust into life we had begun the journey to death.

We realize the futility of trying to escape death even when we are unaware of its nearness. We come close to knowing its meaning in the condemnation that Adam and Eve heard, in the sentence that Jesus heard. Both echo in our own lives. We hear it:

At the death of a grandparent even if we are a very young child.

The first time someone of our own generation dies.

When a person we love moves into eternity.

When our first parent dies.

And, in a special way, no matter what our age, when each of us discovers she or he is an orphan.

In all these moments we know that we, like Jesus, are condemned to die. Because we are Christians, we do not let go of the joy of living today or forget the wonder of knowing life at all. This is resurrection in the midst of day-to-day death.

We pray today for the special grace to live life, fully knowing it will one day end for each of us.

Thoughts for reflection

◀What are some of the experiences of my life that make me aware of the guilt and condemnation felt in the human community?

◀What are some of the ways in which I have "cheapened life"?

◀What can I do in my parish/community/family to affirm life for others?

◀If death comes tonight, what words would I wish I had said today?

THE SECOND STATION
Jesus Is Made to Bear His Cross

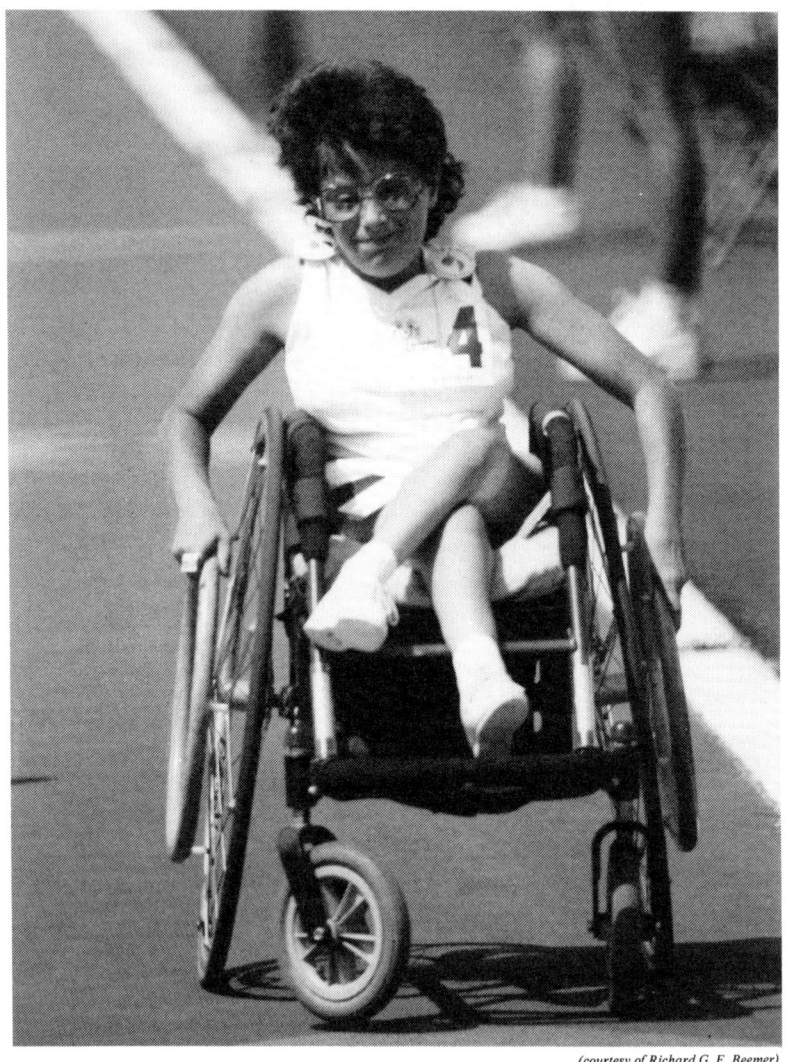

(courtesy of Richard G. E. Beemer)

"So they took Jesus, and carrying the cross himself he went out to what is called the Place of the Skull, in Hebrew, Golgotha."
(John 19:1)

The journey toward death is frequently more painful than death itself. As persons find the significant individuals in their lives wrested from them, they become more and more aware of their own mortality. They discover, too, the power they have within them to carry their burdens.

An earlier translation of the above Scripture passage reads: "...carrying the cross by himself..." This is a most powerful phrase. We are a community. None of us exists alone and for him- or herself. A little reflection makes us aware that our burdens would be heavier were it not for those who share the same vision and values and help us bear the weight of even the heaviest of crosses. This sharing of the load comes in the form of family, friends, and church. Hopefully, it will one day come from the common vision of the total world community.

In whatever form we hear the call to carry our cross, God's People have always known life would not be easy for them. The message is as old as the words spoken by the Father in the Garden of Eden.

"Because you have done this, you shall be banned from all the animals and from all the wild creatures; on your belly shall you crawl and dirt shall you eat all the days of your life. I will put enmity between you and the woman and between your offspring and hers; he will strike at your head while you strike at his heel.

"To the woman he said: 'I will intensify the pangs of your childbearing; in pain shall you bring forth children. Yet your urge shall be for your husband, and he shall be your master.'

> *"To the man he said: 'Because you listened to your wife and ate from the tree of which I had forbidden you to eat, cursed be the ground because of you! In toil shall you eat its yield all the days of your life. Thorns and thistles shall it bring forth to you, as you eat of the plants of the field. By the sweat of your face shall you get bread to eat.'"* *(Genesis 3:14:19)*

Through life, we experience this message in a variety of ways. We discover the most beautiful of roses has thorns. We learn that simply providing for the needs of a family is enough to occupy most parents. Personally, we learn we do not need others to inflict burdens upon us. They are built into our existence.

Even as children, we discovered we had "hardships." For the most part, they were the small disappointments and hurts that came from living in a family and from relating with other children. They were occasions adults seemed to not take seriously. Often, they did not know how badly we were hurt. Slowly, we discovered that hurt feelings did not get nearly as much attention as a scraped knee. We learned, too, that emotional wounds hurt much more than physical ones.

As we approached adolescence, the pain of interpersonal relationships intensified and even a broken leg or appendicitis took second place to loving those who did not return that love or living with the thoughtlessness of persons for whom we cared. Throughout our lives, we have discovered again and again that merely learning what we must know to survive is a hardship itself.

There are those who would justify the hardship of life as the special grace that opens the door to resurrection. Christians sometimes seem to take glory in using the words: "having a cross to bear." Most of us use the phrase before we understand its real meaning. For many generations, we thought that suffering was so ennobling that whatever was without hardship was not worth having.

There are some in the community whose "cross" is obvious to us. We see them suffering with hardship, deprivation, and persecution throughout their lives. Were we to use the "cross" as our excuse for not coming to their aid, we would be misusing the words of Scripture and diminishing the suffering of Christ who came to lighten our burdens rather than make them unbearable.

Most of the time, the ordinary person experiences the cross in small ways and at different times. At those times we look to Jesus and we look toward the community that shares our suffering:

> At times when the life-style we have chosen seems especially burdensome.
>
> On occasions when we are in ill health or mental distress.
>
> When those we love are in pain or troubled.
>
> When we feel friendless.
>
> When we are betrayed.
>
> When we forget that the products of life are born of human toil.

No matter what it is, each of us has something in our life that reminds us we are mortal — that bearing one's cross is the sometimes unhappy facet of facing a life that is on this side of the resurrection.

We pray today for the special grace to accept the crosses we bear at this time in our life. We pray for someone whose cross so permeates his or her life that the person does not know that one day its weight will be lifted by the resurrected Lord.

Thoughts for Reflection

◀What are some of the crosses persons are called to bear simply because they are human?

◀What are some of the crosses the human community is called to lift from the shoulders of those who bear them?

◀What are some of the crosses you have found most difficult to bear during your lifetime?

◀What are some of the burdens you would like to remove from future generations?

◀Whose cross can you help carry today?

THE THIRD STATION
Jesus Falls the First Time

(courtesy of John Zierten)

There is no direct scriptural account of Jesus having fallen on his way to the crucifixion. There are many things not written in Scripture. To get a full picture of Jesus' passion and death, it is necessary to read all the Gospels, and even then there will be some events missing . . . missing because they were part of the ordinary story of those who suffered the sort of sentence Jesus did. After a brutal beating, a night of unbearable anguish, and beneath the weight of the cross, it would have been unusual indeed had Jesus not fallen. Then, the fact would have been recorded. Then the message given by Jesus' suffering would have lacked the element most essential to his followers — he suffered as we suffer.

If our tradition said that Jesus fell only once even that would have been unbelieveable in the light of what we know of the weight of just the crossbeam of the crucifix. Why focus especially on this first occasion of Jesus falling? That first fall, like ours, is particularly significant.

From the moment of our births, our parents and those who love us know we will fall and we will fail. It is they who reach out to kiss our scraped knee and set us on our feet when we first learn to walk. They, too, are the ones who help us rise again as they encourage us (sometimes from the sidelines because of circumstances) when we fail in our efforts at becoming good human persons.

The first fall of any individual or community is significant. First, because it implies a weakness that others might not otherwise recognize. Even referring to it as a first failure implies there will be other falls. We are especially vulnerable when we have never been hurt before. We need encouragement to "pick ourselves up, dust ourselves off, and start all over again." Those who care for us easily see the encouragement we need when the end of our journey holds the hope of success. Those who walked with Jesus, though, knew he was headed toward death. Only a few in that crowd believed his death would be a victory.

The mother of a friend has just begun treatment for what has been called a "terminal" disease. As I watch the family, I feel their torn emotions. They know the suffering she will face, and the odds are clearly not in her favor. As they watch her pain, they are tempted to "let her go." At the same time, they cling to the vibrant will to live she is showing. How much this family is like those who loved the Lord as they watched him on his way of the cross. How unsure they are of what lies at the end of the path.

Most of us can remember neither the first time we fell nor the first time we failed; but, we are much like Jesus. Each time we fail, the wounds already there are deepened and made more painful. This is as true of spiritual failure as it is of physical falling. That first lie can become a web of deceit. The first unkind word can become a pattern of broken relationships.

Think of the small failings in your own life that have become part of the fabric of your existence:

That first infidelity toward a friend.

The first occasion when you exaggerated your importance.

The first time you claimed an unfair deduction on your income tax.

The first time you made an excuse for not having done what you promised.

The first occasion when you blamed someone else for your own failure.

The time you kept silent when you should have spoken.

Communities, like individuals, journey and fall. Support, then, comes from within besides from without. There is no paradigmal account of the first significant fall of God's People in their journey as a community. Instead, we see a history of failures and recoveries continuing through the ages. We could look once more at the Garden of Eden, to Cain and Abel, to the worship of idols, to the Acts of the Apostles which record the failures of the first Christian community.

There are still other failures in the story of the Church today. It is part of being a human community that we fall and that we fail. That this should happen only once as a community is as unbelievable as that Jesus should stumble only once along the way of the cross.

As a Church, we have sacramentalized the need to recognize patterns of failure and recovery in our spiritual life through the Sacrament of Reconciliation. There are times when persons think their failings are too trivial to mention at the Rite. If we were to need to mention them only once, perhaps that would be true; but, with the help of a regular confessor, we can begin to see the ways in which our lives are moving away from the central focus of the Lord by recounting those instances.

The recognition of Jesus' first fall is important for our consideration because we are ever open to first failings that lead to patterns of infidelity.

Let us pray for the special grace to recognize the small infidelities that lead to our separation from the community of the Church.

Thoughts for Reflection

◄What are some of the "firsts" you recognize in the failures of today's world community?

◄Do you see similar "firsts" in your parish/community/city or in the nation?

◄What part do you think you have in those failures?

◄What act or omission today could destroy your relationship with those closest to you in your personal life?

◄Whom do you need in a special way to beg forgiveness from before this day is over?

THE FOURTH STATION
Jesus Meets His Mother

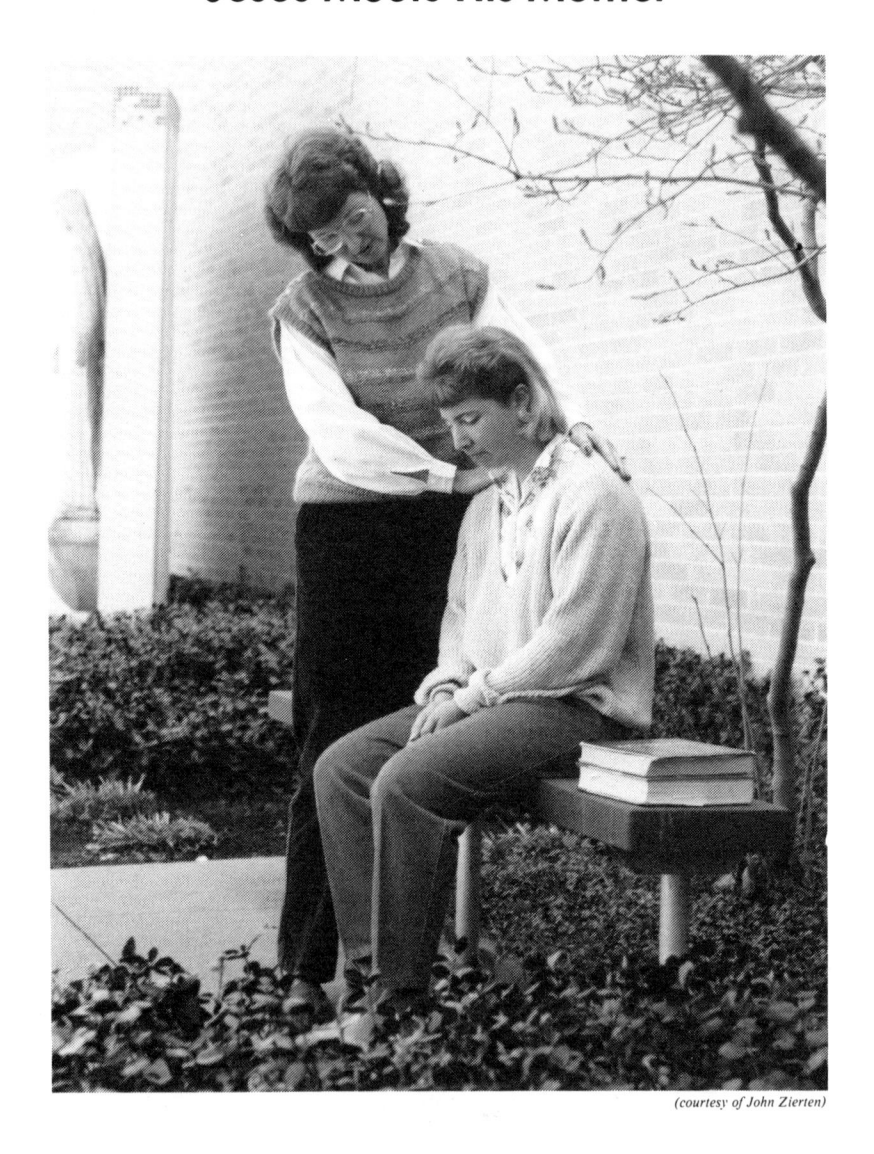

(courtesy of John Zierten)

Stories about Jesus' mother are few in Scripture except on those occasions when she took an active or assertive part; *e.g.*, the Miracle at Cana. Mary was a mother, and she was so integral a part of Jesus' life it is difficult not to imagine her present at significant occasions. Like mothers throughout centuries, she stood next to her son in his agony and wished — as parents always do — that she could bear his suffering for him. And Jesus, like children who remain children to their parents throughout life, undoubtedly wanted to cry out to her with the same passion he used to call on his Father during the Agony in the Garden. Did he, in his pain and humiliation, cry out for his mother? We don't know; but if he did — he was not unlike those through the ages who in pain and trial have called out for the women who gave them birth.

Without a doubt, in spite of the comfort Jesus must have felt in having Mary near, he would have wished that she more than than anyone else, could have been spared the pain of watching him suffer. And, like other mothers throughout all time, Mary undoubtedly wished she could have borne his pain for him during this time.

Throughout the ages, human persons have met their "mothers" in a variety of ways. Some of them have been children whose biological mothers abandoned and rejected them. Their experience of motherhood has come through other nurturing figures, the persons — men and women — who continually offered them life through their support and care on the journey.

The women of the Hebrew Bible tell a story similar to Mary's. Consider Eve for a moment. Here is a woman who loses her son in death. She loses still another son because he has slain his own brother. Who can say for whom she sorrowed more? Imagine Eve's grief at the deaths of her sons — and the double pain of knowing that one had killed the other. What of that moment when Cain faced his parents? Think for a moment of what it must have felt like for them. Consider what that moment was like for Cain. The story doesn't end there.

The story continues through history. It continues through centuries of war whenever mothers watch human brothers kill one another. Consider those who have watched countless caskets return from senseless wars. Think of mothers who watched their children walk into the ovens of Auschwitz and Treblinka. Think, too, of the pain of those who felt the suffering of their mothers even as they walked toward their own deaths. It would be difficult to measure one pain against the other.

Is there one of us who does not know the pain of having our parents witness our failures and our pain? It happens again and again. Our failures and fallings are unique to us as individuals but — somehow — they are the same. Maybe it was:

> A first report card that said we weren't doing as well as we could.

> A time when all of the things our parents worked to give us were things we could not accept.

> A time when a father learned that his son didn't want the family business.

> An occasion when a son or daughter had to tell his or her parents that their grandchild was incurably ill.

There are other experiences, too. There are moments of real and tender love when failure or falling converges with our realization of the depth of our love for our parents.

I recall only too vividly my first thoughts after my mother died. Throughout my life, she had supported my decisions and valued my successes. I often chuckled when I realized she thought I was a much better person than I am. When she died, my first concern was the disappointment she must have felt at knowing me as I am.

As we walk the way of the cross, we continually discover our meditation can take two perspectives: that of Jesus and that of those who related with him. As we meditate on Jesus' meeting with his mother, we can consider the feelings he had and we can concentrate on what Mary felt.

Motherhood is more than a biological reality. It is a call to generativity, a challenge to the world community and to the Church. Those who have no children cannot escape that challenge. Neither do they go unrewarded for the generosity for that sense of generativity and investment in the children of our world.

Throughout the world, children are starving. Some of them are "orphans in our midst." Their starvation is not necessarily physical. Some of them hunger for the love we can give them in a community setting. On occasion, it is only a gentle hug as we tend the scraped knee of the neighbor's child who has fallen while the parents are away. Sometimes, it requires genuine economic sacrifice as we bridle against the financial contribution necessary to keep religious education programs alive and flourishing in our parishes when we have no children of our own.

Our entry into humankind is a commitment to future generations. In truth, it is easier to put that thought aside than to consider the children in our midst who have mothers and fathers but whose parents cannot meet the obligations of nurturing without our assistance.

We pray today with special thanksgiving for the mothers we have met in our lives.

Thoughts for Reflection

◀What obligations do you feel for the children who are physically, psychologically, and spiritually orphaned in this world?

◀What positive action can you take?

◀Who have been the individuals who have nurtured your spirituality and concern for others?

◀Who are those who have parented you on your way of the cross?

◀What would you tell them now if you had the opportunity?

◀If you still can, will you do it?

THE FIFTH STATION
Simon Helps Jesus Carry His Cross

(courtesy of OSV archives)

"As they were going out, they met a Cyrenian named Simon; this man they pressed into service to carry his cross." (Matthew 27:32)

One might wonder what sort of a man Simon was. What was his relationship with the Lord and his motive for action? Did he simply see a need and respond from human compassion? All of us know persons who are able to do that. It is not common in an age when becoming involved in the problems of strangers is likely to make one the victim of a mob or the plaintiff in a lawsuit. Still, there are those who respond.

If Simon lived today, I wonder if he would be one of those working in a soup kitchen or ministering to the dying at the end of his work day. I wonder if he might have succumbed to a modern mentality that would make him content with making tax deductible contributions to social agencies. Would he be concerned about the injustices in the world? Would he care about the hungry and starving oceans away? Would he look with compassion on the Lord and turn away? Even in the world of Simon, his action was a brave one.

Modern media has made us acutely aware of the interconnectedness of human persons. We know isolated self-existence is impossible. We need one another. This need, we quickly discover, extends beyond mere physical interdependence. All of life is a relationship. It is a relationship that causes us pain and a relationship that brings us great joy.

An old adage says, "A friend in need is a friend indeed." It doesn't take us long to discover that we most value those who are with us when we experience both the peaks and valleys of life. We treasure those who are with us at times we would not consider either traumatic or especially joyful. Nonetheless, those who are willing to announce their relationship with us when we are in disfavor with the community hold a special place in our affections.

Throughout the history of God's people, persons from the community have been asked to carry the crosses of others, to help them in service to the Lord, and to bring them toward the fullness of the Kingdom.

> *"Moses said to the Lord, 'If you please, Lord, I have never been eloquent, neither in the past, nor recently, nor now that you have spoken to your servant; but I am slow of speech and tongue.... Then the Lord ... said, 'Have you not your brother, Aaron the Levite?... You are to speak to him, then, and put the words in his mouth... He shall speak to the people for you: he shall be your spokesman, and you shall be as God to him.'"*
>
> *(Exodus 4:10-16)*

This is only one of the stories found in the history of God's People. We hear it again and again in the Hebrew Bible. We hear it in the Gospel in the tale of the Good Samaritan. It has been so throughout the ages.

We are a proud and righteous people. It takes humility to ask for help. It takes even more self-effacement to accept help from others when we don't request it . . . when we think we can carry on by ourselves:

Help from the individual we do not like.

Help from the person for whom we can do nothing in return.

Help from those who make us impatient because we could act more quickly.

Help given grudgingly.

Help given generously.

Help given by the sort of person who will never allow us to forget their aid.

These are issues that face every human person. Today, we recognize them as issues that concern the Church as a community called to witness to Gospel values. As soon as we see this, we become acutely aware that the problems existing in the world are magnified in the Church as we work toward building the community. We are not surprised when non-believers turn against one another or when communities are attacked from outside themselves. That this should happen in the Church itself should not amaze us either.

It is not unusual that those who turn against the prophetic individuals in a community are those within the community itself. There are countless examples of it in the Church today. How painful it is when those who announce the same faith in the risen Lord persecute one another. How painful it is to announce solidarity with those who are persecuted by persons we love. There is no way of avoiding the accusation of "taking sides" with individuals when — if truth be known — we choose to take a stance in regard to an issue rather than a person.

Ours is an age of diversity. It is all too easy to concentrate on the issues that divide us rather than on those which unite us. One wonders what those outside Roman Catholicism think when the modern media focuses on our "family disagreements" and the efforts made to right the injustices we can no longer ignore. On occasion, even the most involved Christian is tempted to think with longing of the days when religion wasn't discussed and when the laity did not think they were entitled to either a voice or an opinion.

The Church formed is the Church that speaks with and for one another even when this is painful. We are a people dependent on one another; but especially needing the combined ministry of other human persons for the Gospel to become rooted in the life of the community. This ministerial solidarity can come only through dialogue and sometimes the dialogue is painful.

Today we ask for the special grace to accept help . . . help we know we need and help we think we could do well without.

Thoughts for Reflection

◄Who in the human community cries out for your help as an individual?

◄Which are the groups that call for community action?

◄Who are the individuals in your own life you would find most difficult to help?

◄Who in this community would be the most difficult for you to approach and say I need you?

◄Could you do it today? Will you?

THE SIXTH STATION
Veronica Wipes the Face of Jesus

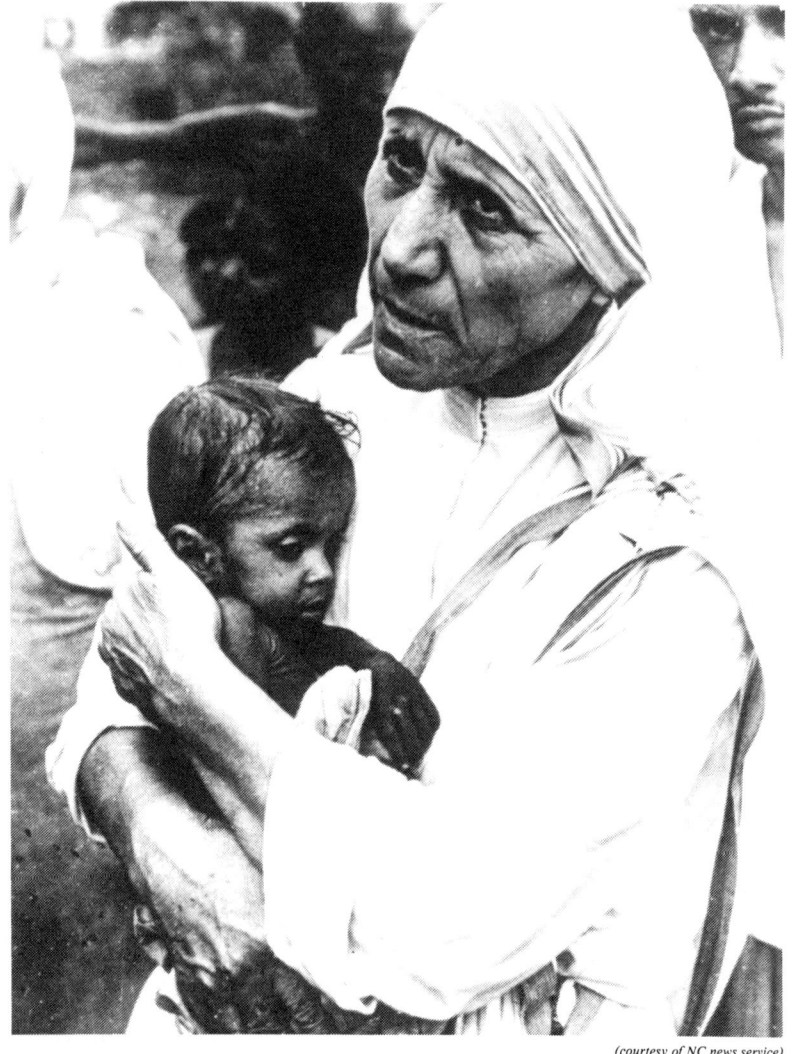

(courtesy of NC news service)

In Jesus' society, a woman was not likely to offer help in the midst of a crowd. Her place was defined by the community. The bravery of a man like Simon defying convention was one thing. A woman offering aid was quite another. One can only imagine the thoughts of those in the crowd as she stepped forward. There were others much closer to Jesus who must have felt envy at her courage. There were those who would have felt outrage at her daring. Those whose adherence to the law rather than its spirit were probably angered that Jesus would — even in his dire need — accept her act of concern. Jesus' face was torn and shredded. The salt of sweat stung the wounds. Veronica was probably not strong enough to help to carry the cross. What could she do? She faced the possibility of being rejected. What could she do? She was a woman, the last person from whom a Jewish man would want help . . . and yet our tradition says he rewarded her by imprinting his face on her cloth.

Deep compassion obscures the possible consequences of one's actions. We have seen it in our own society. We have witnessed it when individuals have confronted mobs determined to violate the rights of an individual. We have heard the stories of those who risk their lives so another might live. Veronica's story is not unfamiliar to us as our own less dramatic stories are told.

There have been persons in our lives who have offered us the only gift they can give . . . themselves. Their actions may well have gone unnoticed and unrewarded by us. We might even have resented their intervention in a situation we thought we could handle without help. Perhaps we were even offended that someone we thought less powerful than ourselves had the ability to come to our aid.

Stories of compassion are woven throughout the Scriptures and in the tradition of the Church. They are part of the story of God's People. Many of them recount the tales of women responding to the needs of those seemingly more powerful than themselves. What of the widow who fed the prophet? What of Mary at the well? What of the countless women who have fearlessly — sometimes while gravely opposed — helped the Church to grow? What of Catherine of Siena? Clare? What of the countless religious women who have educated the active laity of the present? There are also those who witness to us with their lives in less than dramatic ways.

The story of Jesus' having left the print of his face on the cloth that Veronica used is an interesting one from two perspectives. First of all, most of us recognize that persons leave their marks on one another when they relate with each other on this level. Jesus left "himself" with Veronica as we leave ourselves with those who help us when we accept help graciously. Veronica, too, left her mark on Jesus.

The second perspective is more easily seen. When someone acts on our behalf, a dialogue begins and the next word is ours. Jesus said that word is an action. Those who move toward us in love might not expect any reward or response at all. Yet, within us there is a deep need to respond in some way. This simple and sometimes subconscious realization is what makes many reject help from others. They don't want to be "beholden." The more likely truth is they do not want to enter into dialogue or open themselves to a relationship.

One of the oldest pieces of advice in the human community is that to make a friend, you ask them to do something for you. It is equally true that while one cannot "buy" friendship, an act of kindness opens the door of relationships. In both cases, there is an element of risk. We might be rejected in our request and we might be rejected when we offer help. Jesus might well have refused Veronica's aid and Veronica might well have turned away from the implicit request in the suffering eyes of the Savior.

Once initiated, dialogue grows and those relating to one another grow with the relationship. All of us have been marked by numerous individuals who have come to us when we were in need and by those whose need cried out to us. The face of the world has been changed by dialogue. Consider what has happened because of the intervention of countless individuals in the issue of civil rights. Consider, too, the great gaps that must still be bridged to assure these rights to all humans. Will your hand be one that reaches across the chasm that divides the "haves" from the "have nots" in this world?

There is little denying that the Church, too, has been marked by the countless persons who have contributed to its growth. There is still much that must be done. Before the Church can speak with force to the injustice of the world, injustice in the Church itself must be addressed. There are those who will say only the hierarchy has the right and the power to bridge the gaps between what the institution says and what it does. The bishops would be the first to disagree. There are individuals who reject the notion of theological ideas emerging from anyone other than those "authorized" to think. Put into common language, it sounds rather silly doesn't it? The insanity of the suggestion is intended.

Just as compassion cannot emerge from an abstract notion of "world," it cannot come from an abstract idea of Church. We are the world. We are the Church.

Today we pray especially for those who have graced the Church with compassion and suffered for their concern. We pray for those whose care has been rewarded with derision. We pray for those who have reached out to us and to whom we have not responded. Is it too late now?

Thoughts for Reflection

◀Who are the individuals you think have witnessed significantly to compassion in today's world?

◀What have you done as an individual to address the world's needs for compassion?

◀Who has marked your life today?

◀With whom have you left a piece of yourself?

◀What one person would you say has most contributed to your life of faith?

◀Who ought you have touched today and you did not?

THE SEVENTH STATION
Jesus Falls Again

(courtesy of John Zierten)

It was not surprising that Jesus fell again. One might easily meditate on the weakness and suffering of Jesus during this torturous experience. The station says more than that however. The focus is on the strength of Jesus' will to rise again. Physically, the Lord had suffered so much that he could justifiably have resigned himself to giving up. He could easily have died there and redeemed us once and for all. But he did not.

Life is a series of successes and failures. To acknowledge one is to admit the other. Rising the second time takes a different sort of courage than a willingness to get up the first time. It is an admission that there is still more pain to come. This has been the story of humankind throughout history. We have watched nations topple and rise. We have seen people persecuted and defiled only to rebuild their civilizations in the face of what would seem unconquerable odds.

Failure and falling are largely personal stories. We know them well. No matter how hard we try, no matter how good our resolutions, we still fall and we still fail. What of yesterday's mistake that we intensified today? What of the sharp retort we dared give another because she or he was least likely to return it?

We participate, too, in the failures of others. Our very falling causes a chain reaction. There is, for instance, the day when the boss is "on our back" and we take it out on the level below us until the time comes when we arrive home and there is little left to do but figuratively "kick the dog." We see in our own lives what happens when the first of the dominoes topples. Whether it is our unkindness that causes the fall or another's, we fall as a community — but we fall one at a time because of:

The unkind word that multiplied as it passed through the office, the shop, or the factory.

The repetition of yesterday's failure which begins today to establish a pattern.

The little lie of yesterday which became a glaring untruth today.

The injustice that resulted from the words we did not speak before.

The combined failures of humankind make for sad reading without the dimension of renewed effort and greater achievement. The results of this effort are not immediately obvious. It sometimes takes generations to discover its implications. There are times when individuals do not see the results in their own lifetimes. This simple fact causes many to hide their mistakes even from themselves. On the other hand, the courage some individuals have shown in making their mistakes public has often caused the community to look toward them for leadership. Faith in the goodness of life and the redemptive ability of the individual is essential. Without it, these persons might well have left us an impoverished community because of their fear of failure.

We might well be tempted to give up our search for the more spiritually responsive life. We might begin to think about Gospel living as an impossibility. That is the real danger. At times like that, the courage to go on and allow ourselves still one more error is a grace that gives integrity to our lives.

We have seen similar courage in those who surround us. Knowing individuals like this is essential for our own development. To fall "again" is part of our own lives when we have lived long enough. It is part and parcel of the story of God's People. They could have given up countless times. The stories of the Hebrew Bible are familiar to us. We know about the journey through the desert and we know of the hardships of centuries of domination by foreign powers who would force God's people to worship false gods for the sake of comfort and security.

There are failures and fallings that extend into our own generation. Look for a moment at the Jewish community . . . the stories of exile and infidelity. There are newer stories, too. Learn about Masada. Discover the horror of the Russian pogroms, the Balfour Declaration, and the Yom Kippur War.

The story doesn't end with the Bible for the Jewish community; nor, does the Acts of the Apostles recount the last of the Christian tale. There is more to come. As we look at our own Church's history, we can only be amazed at the indomitable courage of those who preceded us. Think of the reformation. Consider our part in the persecution of the Jews. Think of our reluctance to involve ourselves in the sufferings of others and think of the failures of today in which we have a part.

Again and again, the Church has been faced with situations that forced them to choose between the God who revealed himself through Jesus and the god the world held out to them as the answer to their prayers for security and ease. These stories do not end. We hear them in our own day and age. We discover them in the suffering of a bishop courageous enough to tell his flock that he has been to an alcoholic treatment center. We discover them in public church figures willing to admit they have made a mistake in their interpretation of a particular church law. We find them in pastors who ask forgiveness of their parishioners when the occasion demands it. We find it in laity who learn to seek forgiveness of one another even before they ask it of the Church.

We ask for the grace to take our mistakes as opportunities for growth. We pray for the ability to forgive others and to ask their forgiveness. Together, we look at the unkindness and injustice in today's world and Church as our own failures and are challenged to act with the new courage and insight that comes from a willingness to rise once more.

Thoughts for Reflection

◀On what occasions do you think we have — as a human community — not addressed our failures?

◀How as a Church do you think we have fallen and not risen?

◀What are the parts of your past you have not addressed in this way?

◀What are the failures you see in your life today?

◀What can you do to rise from your failings?

THE EIGHTH STATION
Jesus Meets the Women of Jerusalem

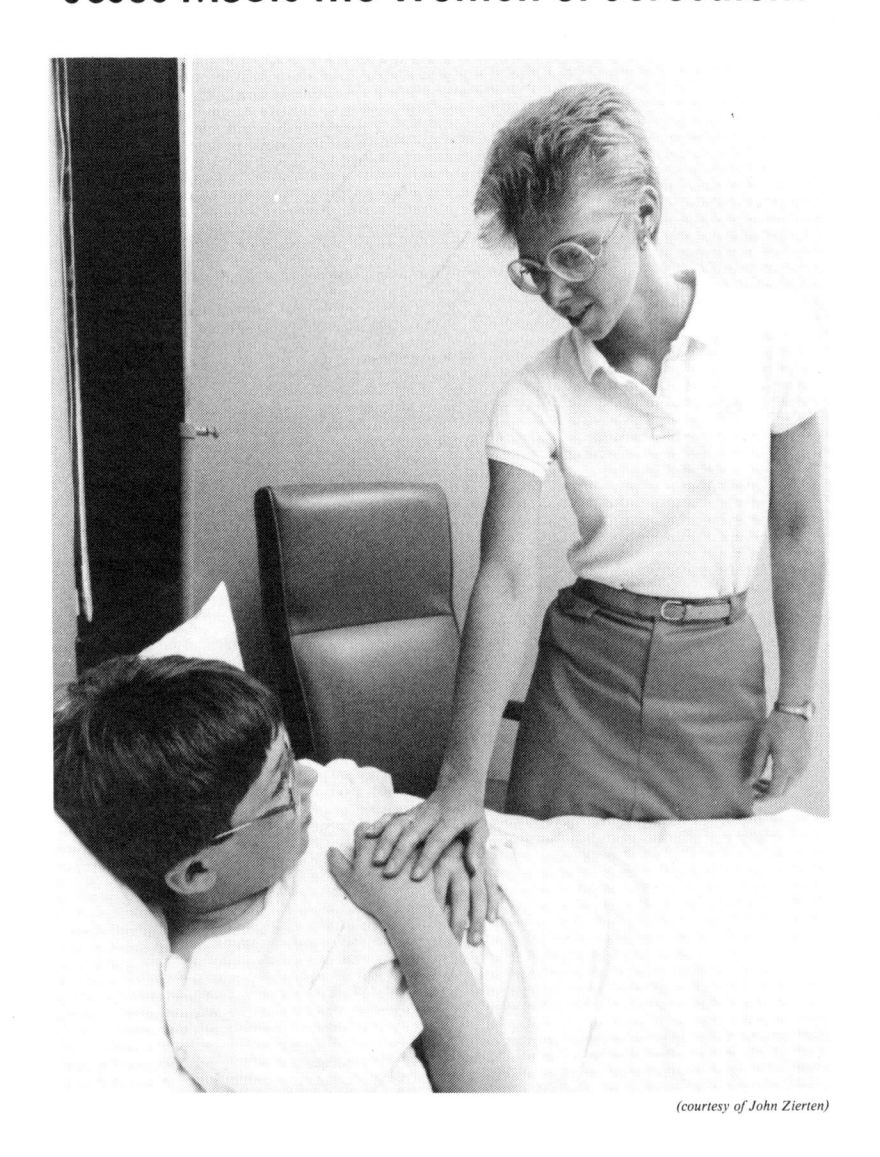

(courtesy of John Zierten)

"A large crowd of people followed Jesus, including many women who mourned and lamented over him."
(Luke 23:27)

"Standing by the Cross of Jesus were his mother and his mother's sister, Mary the wife of Clopas, and Mary of Magdala."
(John 19:25)

"But at daybreak on the first day of the week the women took the spices they had prepared and went to the tomb."
(Luke 24:1)

Why the special emphasis on the place of women during Jesus' passion and crucifixion? Until the time of Jesus, women were not a legitimate part of the community. When the size of a crowd was estimated, women would not even be counted. If their opinion was sought, it was only in the confines of the home. Their very existence was defined by their marriage and the birth of a son. In the rabbinic tales, women do not emerge as heroines. Yet, oddly enough, they come to the fore again and again in the Hebrew Scripture. If the women of Jesus' time had been encouraged to know the women who preceded them, they might well have occupied a different place in the history of the time.

There is no denying they are signficant throughout Jesus' ministry and central to whatever support he had during his passion. Officially recognized or not, the ministry of women in the formation of God's people has a history of its own rooted in persons like Deborah, Sara, and a Pharaoh's daughter who raised Moses as her own.

Discrimination against women is not confined to religion. Only a little awareness of the establishment of American government reveals a history of the violation of the dignity of women completely in keeping with the precedent set throughout ages in countries other than our own. What women signed the Declaration of Independence? Which one was consulted about the Constitution of the United States? Ought American women be satisfied with exalting in Betsy Ross who sewed a flag? This does not imply that if the tales were told with accuracy we would not find countless heroines in the establishment of American democratic principles. That our children are not taught those women's accomplishments speaks more about those who wrote the history than those who lived it.

American women have made giant strides. None of us, though, is willing to be content with a grudging acknowledgment that we are entitled to basic human rights unless those rights extend to the ability to help shape and form the visions and values of the land in which we live. The need for women of vision to speak loudly and clearly is as essential today as it was during the time when women of the past struggled out of the sweatshops and toward the voting booth. The fault is not only in the male society. Many women fear the responsibility of being responsible for themselves. It gives them little courage to think about the "hidden responsibility" they must bear for individuals with whom they are related.

Our responsibilities are not confined to those who live in the United States. In many Latin and European countries, offenses against the dignity of women are rampant. Girl infants are left to die in the streets. The laws for women are different from the laws for men. Where does our responsibility lie in those cases? How strange that the United States should so easily involve itself in the policy of foreign nations when the issue is ultimately economic and, yet, not speak out for the oppressed when it is not.

The situation in religious institutions is similar. We live in a Church where discrimination against women is a matter of record. There are still those — and women among them — who will move to a different communion line when they discover a woman distributing the Eucharist. The question of women's rights in the Church is larger than theological musing about whether or not women can be priests. It is broad enough for us to wonder what might happen to the ministry of the Church today if women removed themselves from the roles of Directors of Religious Education, principals and teachers in our Catholic schools, and from the many hidden ministries in parishes large and small.

From time to time, the Holy Father and a large number of bishops issue letters and documents praising the contributions of women in the Church. Yet, how much have we really changed? How willing are we to acknowledge the place of women in the Church today? Women as well as men are responsible for this injustice. What subtle forms of persecution and discrimination are part of our own lives?

There is no denying that throughout history, women have had little to say about the decisions of world or Church; but, it is to them we have turned for consolation. They are the ones who literally nurse the children, bury the dead, and comfort those who are bereaved. Who are the women in your life:

Who witnessed to the possibility of fidelity?

Who held you when you hurt?

Who told you that they loved you and made you believe it?

Whose presence you did not acknowledge today?

Whose loving care you took for granted?

Whose ambition and progress you resented?

Think of the women in your life to whom you have turned for consolation. Think of those who would not take it amiss if you called them in the middle of the night for solace. We pray for those women today and ask for the grace not to be part of a society that denigrates their contribution. We remember in a special way that Jesus was a human being, a man, and that he, like all normal human men, loved women — celibately and chastely — but, nonetheless, loved women. Scripture is filled with that love.

We pray for those women who have the courage to minister to the needs of God's people in the midst of oppression and do not abandon the call to that ministry when it is not appreciated or valued.

Thoughts for Reflection

◀How is your life different from that of your grandmother or great grandmother?

◀Do you really believe in the ability of a woman to contribute to the world? the Church?

◀How has a woman helped you grow?

◀What "womanly" quality do you have that you would like to give to the world?

THE NINTH STATION
Jesus Falls the Last Time

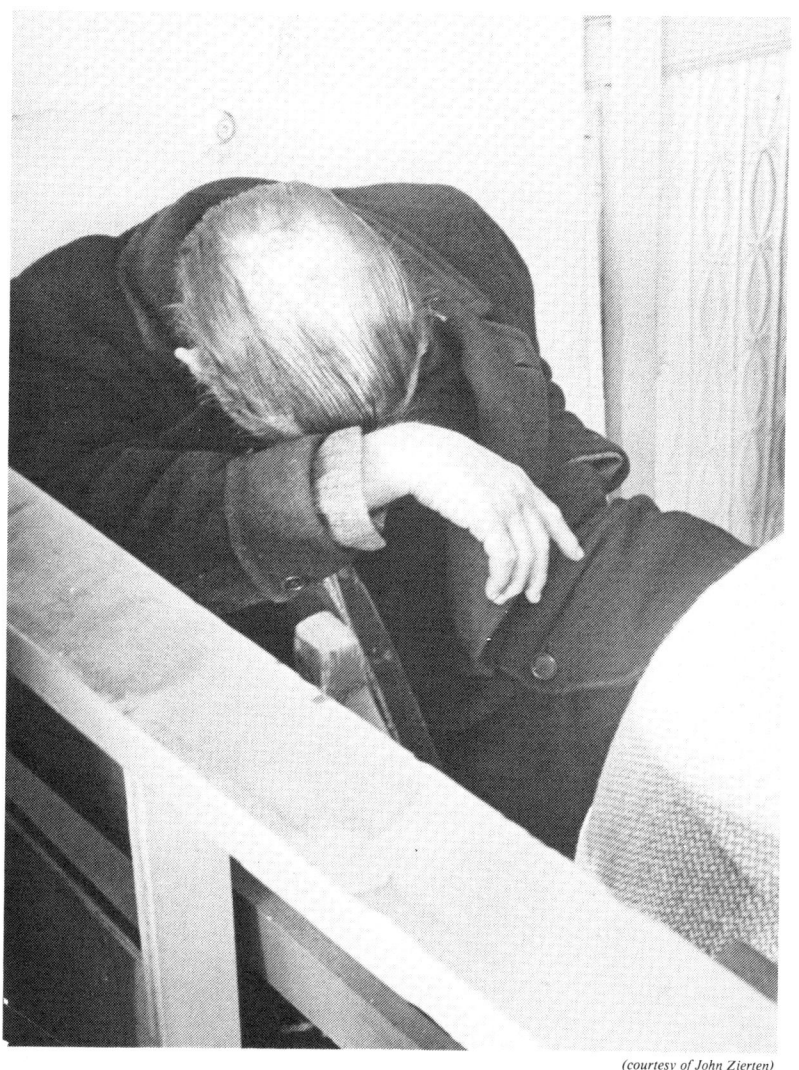

(courtesy of John Zierten)

There is a reason for this station being called "Jesus falls the last time" rather than the third time. We should not assume that Jesus fell only three times along the way toward crucifixion. He may have fallen many more times. He might have staggered and reeled many times and been pushed back on his feet by the rabble. What is important is that even when he fell the "last time," he rose again. He simply did not give up in spite of hardships. One might easily ask what gave him the courage? He was sustained by the faith he had in the Father. He had his eyes on the goal. Each step was taken because he knew the reason for the hope he had. He was also motivated by the same thing that helps many of us carry on in spite of difficulty — the faith of those who stood with him. One dimension of his faith was in the community, the belief of Simon, of Veronica, of his Mother, and the faith of those who did not have the courage to step forward.

One wonders how even those most opposed to his message could ignore his courage and ask questions about his motivation. Surely, many must have been convinced that if they were in his place, they would have given up after going only a little way toward what would be the final ignominy. Time and again, catechumens will point to the courage they have seen in individual believers in the midst of seemingly impossible situations as their reason for looking at the Church in a new light. They look for entry into a community whose faith in human life will provide a context for the hope that lies dormant in their own hearts.

All of us know there will be a "final fall" in our lives. Our prayer is that we will rise and move once more toward resurrection. In no sense, is death a fall. It is a moment toward which we hope to move with integrity and faith. Perhaps, though, the final fall is the one that concerns us most. We do not know the form our death will take. Will we face months of pain and physical suffering? Will we be alone? Will there be anyone who will care that we are leaving them? Jesus' final fall is a message to the Christian community. It is one all of us will one day be in a position to contemplate whether because of the length of our days, the seriousness of an illness, or simply because we realize our own mortality.

One of our fears is that our "final fall" will cause us to lose faith and we will simply say: "I've had it. I will not try anymore. This is more than I can bear" or "I cannot be better than I am now." Jesus did not do that. In pain and anguish, he lifted himself again and continued to carry the cross that had been placed upon his shoulders.

None of us chooses his or her cross. We do not deliberately set out upon a path of pain or of temptation. But anguish and trial are part of the human condition. One of the dangers of looking at the Stations of the Cross apart from the totality of life is their intensity. In a very short time, we can take passion and pain out of the context of life and forget the goodness of the life we treasure. We can remember only the situations that cause anxiety and forget the underlying faith we have in the resurrection. We can lose sight of the very things that help us overcome our trials.

Most of us know — even as we resolve to do better — that we have not fallen the final time. We know there are other hardships we will have to face and we know we may even fail in the same way again. Although we do not know the pressures in store for us the rest of this day, this week, or this month, we know that it is the nature of life they will come. At those times when we are able to speak with courage it is because of the hope underlying our very being. We make our resolution for "now" even though we have serious concern about our future.

Jesus is the symbol of the total People of God. The way of the cross "liturgizes" the past and future of these people. In the fidelity of the Jewish community and its consistent effort to keep its covenantal promises, we see a reflection of God ever ready to "lift" his people . . . people who fell again and again. Throughout the Hebrew Bible, Yahweh is there. In the story of our Church, from the time of the first Christian community, the Risen Christ walks with his people.

There have been many falls and failings in the history of our Church. Time and again, individuals have seen the failings of our human community and said, "I will no longer believe in this community." No one has ever left the Church because Jesus has betrayed them. Countless, though, look at individuals — clergy and laity — who represent the Church and see their failures as a reason for not believing in Roman Catholicism. Certainly that number would be multiplied if those who were Roman Catholic wore a public sign of their faith as they sat in boardrooms, shopped in supermarkets, and drove the highways. All of us are painfully aware of the gaps between our faith and our actions. That is what most of our spiritual failures concern. Most of us — because of the grace of the sacraments — rise again; but, too many of us are responsible for others who fail because they fall and we do not help them to rise.

Who today could have looked at you and said, "If that is the Church, I want to know more about what it is to believe in Jesus"? Who could have seen your actions and said, "If that is a believer, it is not what I want"?

Meanwhile, personally aware of our limitations, we strive to live the Gospel. And we fall again and again. Often it is the encouragement of others like ourselves that enables us to continue on the path of resurrection. Like Jesus, we find individuals on the fringes of the crowd whose faith helps us to continue. There are persons who love us enough to help us rise again. There are times, too, when we do this for them. We see the low spirits of others and reach out to give them some of the courage we might have at that particular moment. We are invested in one another, bound together by the visions and values brought to us through Jesus and nourished by our sacramental life.

We pray in a special way for those whose faith we have weakened because we have not allowed them to rise once more when they have fallen, or because we have led them to believe, in a moment of our own weakness, that we will not rise again. We pray for the courage to rise again ourselves when it would be far more comfortable to simply luxuriate in feeling discriminated against or deprived.

Thoughts for Reflection

◀What does this station say to you at this time in your life?

◀What are some of the situations which seem unbearable to you now?

◀Have you recently given in to the discouragement of yet another rebuff?

◀When have you fallen and allowed yourself to be consoled but have not risen?

◀When have you wallowed in your weakness rather than rejoiced in your strength?

◀What hope can you give to those in your family and community who are surrounded by hardship? Who have fallen and look to you for help in rising?

THE TENTH STATION
Jesus Is Stripped

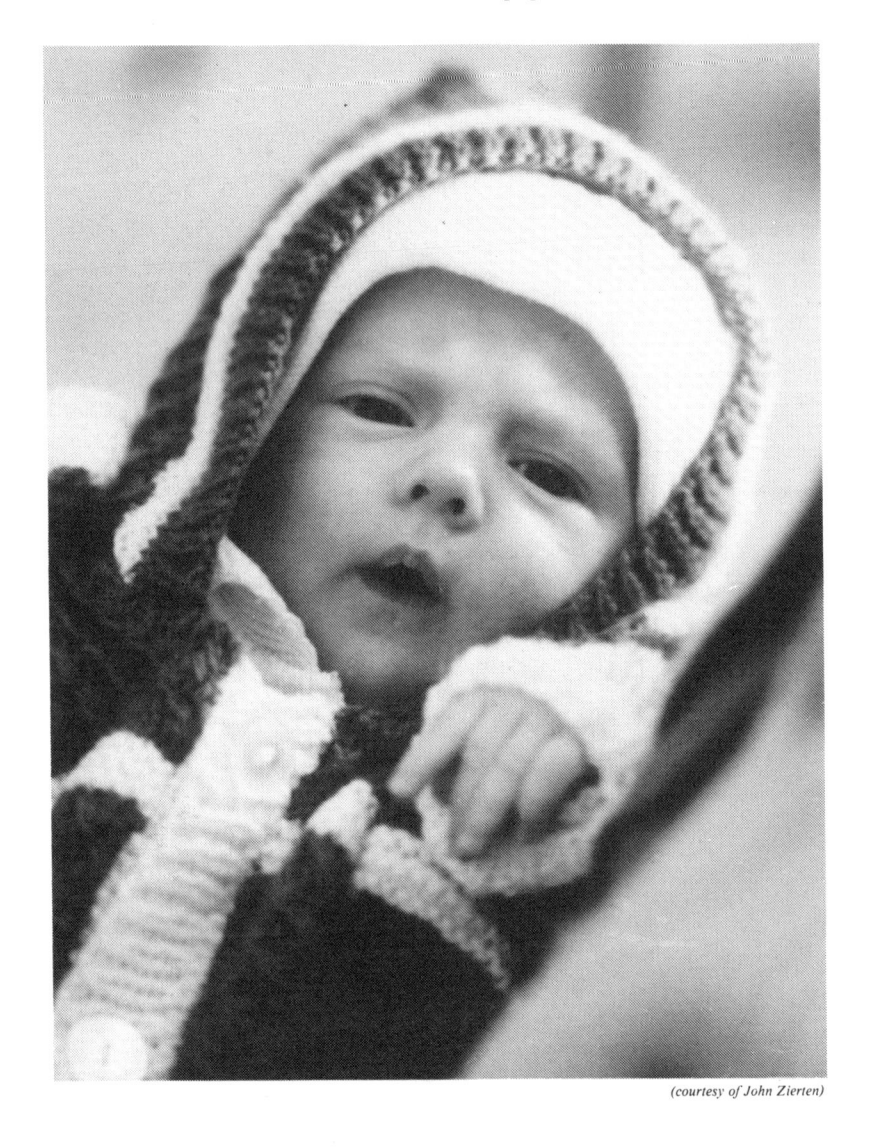

(courtesy of John Zierten)

"After they had crucified him, they divided his garments by casting lots."

(Matthew 27:35)

From an early age, most of us discover that our clothing matters. It makes a difference to us and it is something which others notice. A history of fashion and clothing fads reveals much about the values of a particular time. Eve's first concern might have been to cover herself physically; but, I suspect it wasn't long before she began to vary her attire.

We come naked and without shame from the wombs of our mothers. Even before we were born, our parents were planning what we would wear. It makes little difference to a new mother that an infant doesn't care. Infant garments reveal much about those who clothe us. As we mature, our clothing begins to reveal more than it conceals. Subconsciously, we dress both for ourselves and for others. Our attire tells the world what we want it to know. It becomes one of the ways in which we are able to hide. It sets up an image for the world. It helps us identify with a group and it helps the group accept us. Consider for a moment the teen years when looking like the crowd is important. When Catholic schools began to phase out high school uniforms, teens adopted their own.

The importance of the way we dress does not end with our adolescence. The executive seeking a job with a new company, for instance, determines before his interview if this is a "gray flannel," three-piece-suit corporation or if it is part of the denim crowd. He dresses according to the standards of the company even if the style is not his. The woman concerned about her status as an "executive" easily finds herself drawn to suits even if she might prefer a softer look. In some areas of the country, local people can identify the area of the city from which persons come simply by looking at the way they are dressed.

Somehow, though, we are never able to completely hide. Even if the world does not know us for who we are, we know and we are aware that the time will inevitably come when we will wittingly or unconsciously drop the mask behind which we hide.

"And Job said: 'Naked I came forth from my mother's womb, and naked shall I go back again. The Lord gave and the Lord has taken away.' " (Job 1:21)

Part of the process of revealing ourselves comes when we develop relationships of love and friendship. We are affirmed when there are individuals in our lives who have seen us just as we are. Their ability to accept us physically enables us to share our ideas and to make our faith transparent. Still, there will always be those individuals with whom we are unable and unwilling to share. To figuratively stand "naked" and stripped of our defenses is difficult when we choose it. It is far more abhorrent when we do not have the choice. Jesus did not choose his nakedness and he had nothing to hide.

Growing in faith is a process of revelation. It is easy in the world of the Church to get caught up in the trappings. We look, for instance, at the Eucharistic liturgy and often think about its values in terms of the homily preached or the music chosen. Worship with one another is successful when it enables us to make our faith transparent to those who worship with us and to carry that transparency to the world. The real attire of faith is found in the lives we live and the actions we perform in the name of the Lord. To judge liturgy by any other standard is to "clothe" it in a garb it was never meant to wear.

All of prayer is like that. When we gather with our families and spontaneously pray about what concerns us, we reveal that faith we have not only in ourselves but in the persons with whom we gather. When those who believe in one another pray, they know the Lord has placed the power to answer prayer in the community. In the intimacy of a home, for instance, even as one individual prays the others consider how they can help that prayer be answered.

Even if we do not choose it, all of us will come to the time when we will stand stripped and naked before a world that accuses us. The process has already begun. We have, for instance, lost our illusions about war. No longer do most hide behind the fairy tale that force will give us all we seek. We have begun to take responsibility for the impoverished and for the victims of injustice. Yet, we have not regained our real innocence. Again and again, we are victimized by a society that says image is everything and saving face with the world even at the cost of human life is more important than integrity.

Because we know the evil within ourselves, we know the possibility of evil among others. We know the terror of nuclear war, but we fear to embrace nuclear disarmament lest the power of Satan might possibly overcome the goodness of humankind. We have lost that holy innocence that is not mere naiveté. Many wear another sort of innocence and self-righteousness as a protective garment, an armor against whatever guilt they might otherwise feel.

From the Garden of Eden, we have known the shame and the fear of being naked. We learn through life that our bare bodies are not what really causes our embarrassment. What we most fear is showing the world the sort of persons we really are. Revealing ourselves with our faults and failings frightens us. We try to hide what is evil within ourselves and — at the same time — obscure our goodness. If others know our faults, they will value us less. If they know our goodness, their expectations might be too high for us to meet them. We value too highly the esteem and expectations of the human community.

Today we pray for the grace to show ourselves to someone who can help us to accept our nakedness and help clothe us once more with the pride that Jesus gives us in his willingness to bare himself before us.

Thoughts for Reflection

◀What does your manner of dress say about what you want others to think about you?

◀What sort of "garb" does the United States wear to project an image?

◀What does the liturgy in your parish say about how the parish sees itself?

◀Who are the persons from whom you have hidden today?

◀What goodness have you obscured?

◀How have you failed to allow others to help you because you would not let them see your weakness?

THE ELEVENTH STATION
Jesus Is Nailed to the Cross

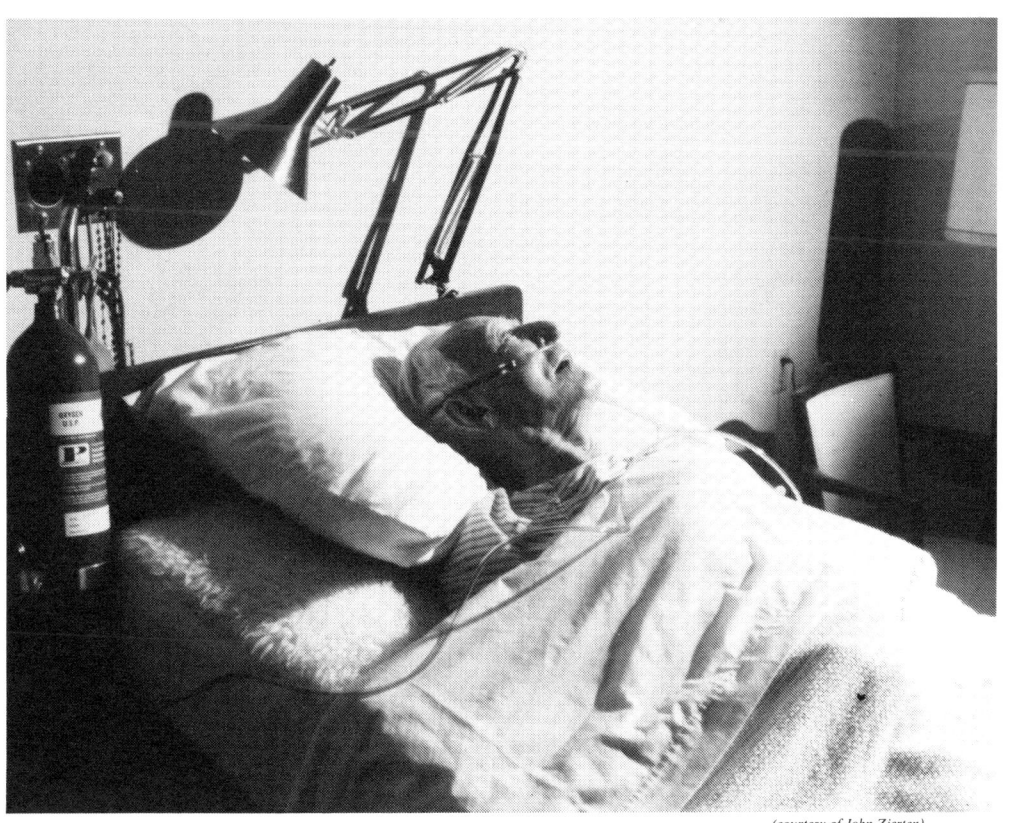

(courtesy of John Zierten)

"When they came to the place called the Skull, they crucified him and the criminals there..."

(Luke 23:33)

Death is a reality none of us can escape. From the moment of birth, we subconsciously begin the process of grief over the loss of our life. We shed tears over the loss of baby teeth as we move toward childhood, the loss of our innocence as we become adolescents, the loss of our friends as we mature, the loss of our parents. In some way, each of these is ultimately grief for ourselves. We experience our own deaths again and again. Most of our sorrow is spread throughout a lifetime without our ever knowing it. Consequently, the matter of dying is not as much a trauma for us as the thought of how we will die and sorrow for those who will remain behind.

Death is the ultimate sign of our powerlessness. We do not have even the power to choose the manner of our dying. Will we suffer for months or die suddenly in an accident? Will we die with dignity? This has been a question of growing concern in a society where medical advances have enabled individuals to linger for months or even years without being able to control even their own thoughts. While we are not likely to die in a way even remotely as horrible as Jesus, there are other deaths that can strip our last moments of the dignity with which we were born.

Our concern about death is not limited to a personal one. Most persons experience the impact of death through the loss of an individual they love. We care not only about their death but the way in which they die. As we mature, we grow in our concern about the ways in which all individuals die. The concern we have for human life leads us to become involved in right-to-life issues like abortion and euthanasia. It leads us to address the issue of alcohol and drugs, to establish hospices, and to work with ever-increasing diligence to overcome disease and disablement. One of the greatest gifts given us through Jesus' incarnation is the path he walked in life knowing itultimately would lead to death. None of us need ever be ashamed to die. Jesus died in the most horrible manner. Even when our death lacks the dignity we would most desire, we can look to the Lord who walked that path before us.

Death, for most, is a natural process. It comes through sickness, through accident, and simply because we have lived our allotted time. This is not, though, true for everyone. Each day we learn of an increase in the suicide rate among the very young. We hear of those whose vision of the world is distorted by the evil they see and simply do not consider life worth living.

There are still other individuals throughout the world who are tortured and persecuted for their faith. Jesus' death has a different meaning for them.

History treats martyrs kindly. Those who die at the hand of an assassin often achieve a kind of immortality they would not ever have were it not for the manner of their death. Many individuals are remembered as having died for a cause even when their lives do not reflect a faith deep enough for them to have willed death. Put simply, dying at the hand of another is not a great achievement. It is significant that Scripture recounts the fact that Jesus died with criminals. With whom we die, it seems, is as important as the manner of our death. Those who plotted to kill the Lord knew this. Every effort was made to justify the death and to plant a mental association in the minds of those who observed it. Even in that age, they knew the danger of having Jesus appear a martyr.

In today's world, there is a similar mentality in those countries where persons face death because of the stand they take against injustice. No country is willing to face the turmoil and rebellion resulting from admitting to the persecution of others because of their faith. Instead, mock trials are held and charges fabricated. Criminal actions are cited rather than the underlying reasons.

The horror of Nazi death camps was never fully revealed until the atrocity was well under way. There are those who would say such a thing could not happen again. Yet, *Shoah* — a modern film examining the attitudes of those who lived during that time — easily convinced the viewer that it could happen. That it does not is a matter of conscience for the entire world. All of us carry the guilt of that period of history just as we share in the guilt of those who crucified the Lord.

As individuals and as a community, we share in the actions of all humankind. The atrocities of others are as much a shame to us as the achievements of those who conquer disease or advance the sciences in other parts of the world are a source of pride. Each individual weakens or strengthens the human community. The goodness of the human community is the responsibility of each of us.

Throughout the history of the world and the Church, there have been thousands of persons whose death echoes Jesus' death in a variety of ways. These are those who have died in ignominy and seemingly without reason. They are the prophets who have been stoned, the martyrs, those who have died from greed or by the hand of an assassin.

"They threw him out of the city, and began to stone him. . . . As they were stoning Stephen, he called out, 'Lord Jesus, receive my spirit.' " (Acts 7:58-59)

"About that time King Herod laid hands upon some members of the church to harm them. He had James, the brother of John, killed by the sword. . ." (Acts 12:1-2)

It is not likely that death will come like that for any of us. Yet, violent, unnecessary and tragic death comes into our daily lives with the evening news and with the morning newspaper. Each day we learn of new victims of assassins and those who would use violence for power. In the ghettos of our large cities, many will meet death violently tonight and it will be so common it will not appear on the news.

At this moment, there are persons plotting the death of diplomats and heads of state. Violence is a way of life in many Latin American countries. We pray for those who are the victims of others who would plot their deaths at this moment . . . persons in Latin America, in Asia, in Europe, in Africa, and in the ghettos of our large cities. We pray for the repentance of those who will bring pain to others and for courage for those who must bear that pain.

Thoughts for Reflection

◀How do violence and aggression in modern society affect society's value of life?

◀What are the "little deaths" that have helped prepare you for your own future?

◀What experience in your life has made you most aware of your own mortality?

◀Is Jesus' death or his resurrection more real to you? Why do you think this is so?

◀What can you do to help the next generation cherish life?

◀When you think of your own death, what emotions do you feel? What are your greatest concerns?

THE TWELFTH STATION
Jesus Dies on the Cross

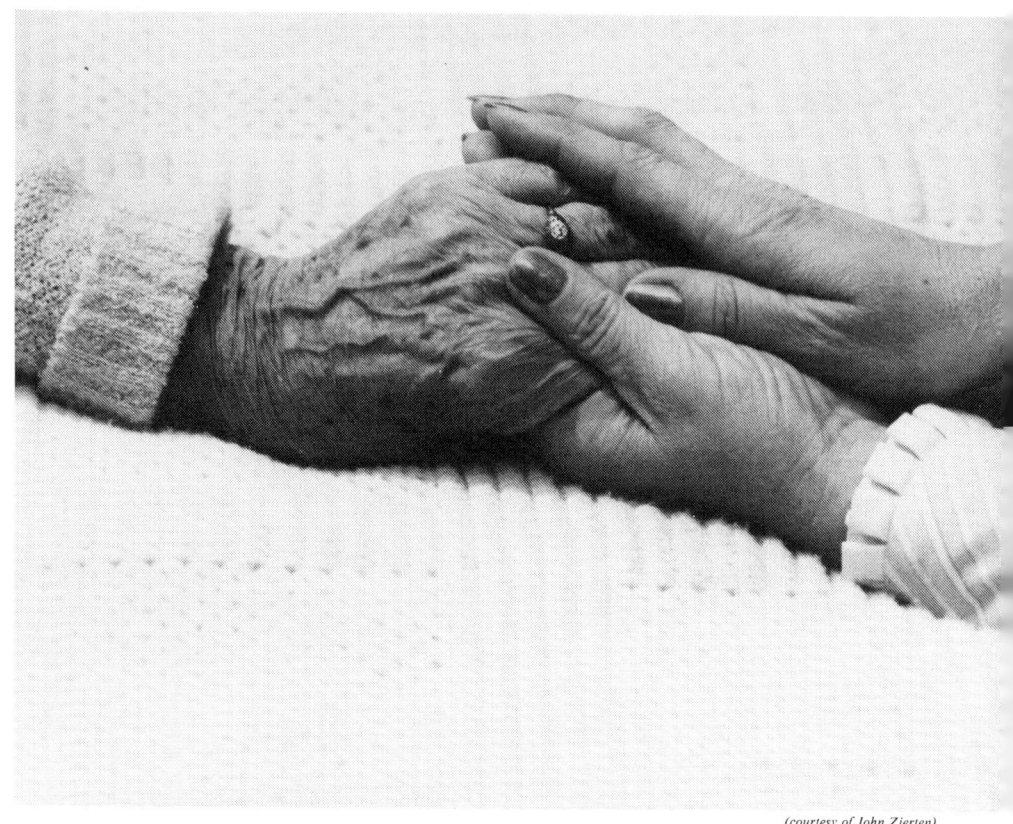

(courtesy of John Zierten)

"When Jesus had taken the wine, he said, 'It is finished.' And bowing his head, he handed over the spirit."
(John 19:30)

Death walks with us every step of the way as we walk the way to Jesus' resurrection and our own. For every person in history, there is a similar story. It is their story and it is ours. Should we speak of the death of Moses? recount the story of how Jeremiah dies? or Peter? or Stephen? or any of our modern martyrs? or should we speak of the death of our best friends? These are the stories we tell throughout our lives. Sometimes, though, we do not consider the ultimate "letting go" associated with death. Like Jesus, each of us at some time is called to not only accept but almost to will our death and the separation from those we love. More important, we need to know they are willing to let go of us.

When my mother developed an infection, it seemed she would recover. My family and the doctor were optimistic. In only two days the situation changed. I remember, though, the first morning when I brought her into the emergency room and made her promise to get well. She shook her head in affirmation and I relaxed. I remember her struggling for life in those days and night hours as we sat in the intensive care waiting room. Then came the moment when the doctor said she would not recover; but, her death would not be that night. All of us should go home and rest so we could better deal with the decisions we would have to make the next day. Somehow, I felt there was something else we had to do first. My brother, my sister, my niece, and I gathered at her bedside. Each of us told her we loved her. We prayed and then, one by one, each of us told her it was all right. We told her she could let go. My teenaged niece said it best: "It's okay, Granny, you can go ... but hang on if you want to." We prayed again and — not even certain she had heard us — we left the room. In less than thirty minutes she died. Suffering as she was, I was certain she was waiting only for our permission and assurance that she need not fight death for our sakes.

The loss of those we love is confrontation with our own mortality; but, at first, it is — more than anything — a profound and deep emptiness. My mother, I think, knew that and needed the assurance we would be with one another to fill the gap left in our lives.

When death gives those who love one another the opportunity, there are rituals that need to be accomplished. Sometimes we think of it only as the making of a will and the arrangements for burial. More important, it is preparation of those we love for separation and helping one another accept what is coming.

"When Jesus saw his mother and the disciple there whom he loved, he said to his mother, 'Woman, behold, your son.' Then he said to the disciple, 'Behold your mother.' And from that hour the disciple took her into his home." (John 19:26-27)

Jesus' actions were a sign of his "letting go" and an encouragement to his mother to accept what was coming. Throughout the way of the cross he had "hung on" and struggled for life as all of us do. Then, when he knew his hour had come, he looked toward those who would most feel his absence and entrusted them to one another. There is no scriptural account of Mary's response. Perhaps she wept. Maybe she needed to be alone. Perhaps John held her in his arms. She, too, knew the hour had come. He had accomplished all there was for him to do and he could "deliver over his spirit." This is the greatest sign of the dignity he bore even though they had tried to strip him of his humanity. Jesus willed his own death. It was not merely something done to him. Many of us will have to face this sort of ritual in the death of one we love or in our own death.

Family planners and financial advisers speak often about the need to be ready for death by providing for the economic needs of those for whom we are responsible. Unfortunately, most persons do not take the same loving care when dealing with the emotional needs of those who love them.

It is important for persons who love one another to talk about what it would mean emotionally and spiritually to lose one another. What are the concerns we have for each other? What are the worries we have about ourselves? Those who refuse to talk about death are dealing with it anyway. They are taking options away from themselves and from others. When we are gone, we do not have the ability to comfort those who love us. Just as we begin to deal with death within ourselves from the moment of birth, the process of comforting the community should be lifelong.

We don't know the time when we will die. We don't know the hour. It doesn't make any difference:

Some of us will die with dignity. Others will not.

Some will fall asleep one evening and simply not awaken.

Some will have months or even years of pain.

Perhaps we will die this evening.

Maybe we have years before us.

It is important for us to know that death, though certain, is always a surprise. Deep within us, each has an intuition that she or he will live forever. The intuition is rooted in the reality of resurrection. The danger is that we might direct it toward a feeling of immortality instead. Those who have been promised the gift of life in its fullness for all of eternity ought not be satisfied with what is second best: immortality.

We pray that no matter what the manner of our death, we will embrace it as a step into the future. Today we think with special love and prayer of someone who is dying and has no one with him or her on that journey. We consider those who will be pained when we are gone and those whose absence will bring us pain. The gift we can give them now is dialogue about that time and comfort and healing for the time when they will need that care. We can do as Jesus did and entrust them to one another. This is the time when we begin to "let go."

Thoughts for Reflection

◀When have you most felt powerless about death?

◀What are some of the events of your life that remind you that you do have something to do with the way you will die?

◀Who are the persons about whom you will be most concerned should you die this evening?

◀Who are the individuals with whom you should speak about death?

◀How can you let go of life and choose greater life today?

THE THIRTEENTH STATION
Jesus Is Taken Down From the Cross

(courtesy of OSV archives)

> *"Pilate was amazed that he was already dead. He summoned the centurion and asked him if Jesus had already died. And when he learned of it from the centurion, he gave the body to Joseph."*
> *(Mark 15:44-45)*

There is little doubt that Pilate was eager to have the body of Jesus removed. He had no wish to hold Jesus in his arms. Had he witnessed the way of the cross, he would not have been surprised that Jesus had died. He would have been amazed he had endured so much. But there was no escape for Pilate any more than we can escape the presence of death in our midst. Death touches us at every moment. We cannot simply "release the corpse" anymore than Pilate could.

Pain is the legacy left by those who love us and those whom we love. For each of us there is a moment when another person's pain is passed on to those who love him or her. Perhaps it happens when the doctor says: "She is gone," or when the telephone rings to say that one's friend, mother, father, wife or husband is dead. If not literally, the person is — at that moment — placed in our arms and, like Mary, we hold him or her. Those who have known this experience see their own reflection as they view the Pieta. This is undoubtedly one of the reasons for the powerful emotions persons feel when they see this work of art.

As surely as Jesus entered into the fullness of our human experience, he entered this one, too. Even this experience he did not spare himself. We feel it in the powerful story of Lazarus. Jesus loved Lazarus. His sorrow and loss were apparent. He knew that psychological and spiritual moment of holding the body of the one he loved in his arms. Picture him in Mary's place. Like his Mother and like us, Jesus wept. The raising of Lazarus was not an effort on Jesus' part to escape having to let go. Neither was this Jesus' only experience. What grief he must have felt at the loss of Joseph, the man who parented him through childhood. Through these experiences the Lord blessed the experiences we would have in our own lives. Through them he taught us how to live.

On countless occasions throughout life, we are called to hold the dead body of someone we love:

In an intensive care unit of a hospital.

In the doorway of a skid row tavern.

Amid the flowers of a funeral home.

Over the telephone and by way of a telegram.

That we do not always receive the body physically makes little difference. As surely as we are born to love, we are destined to fill our arms with the sign of our loss.

We are called to receive the bodies of those in whose death we have had a part. Because we are part of humankind, we share not only its glory but its failure. We cannot escape our passive part in the atrocities of World War II or our responsibility in the deaths of countless young men throughout centuries of war. There is no way we can avoid receiving the bodies of those killed in the ghetto or even those who take their own lives because of our failure to communicate that life is to be cherished.

There are times when the entire world is asked to hold those bodies in their arms. Each time a military transport arrives with the body of another victim of a senseless war, the entire country receives it and shares the grief and guilt for the one who has died.

Throughout the centuries and even today, those who die for their faith have been placed in the collective arms of the Church. Even while we glory in their resurrection and the life they have in Christ, we deplore the senselessness of death because of persecution.

Sometimes death is merely a natural movement from life to fuller life. Still the moment is painful and the process of feeling the risen presence of the one we loved is lengthy. There comes a time, too, when we must surrender the body and choose to live either with emptiness or allow the community to console us. Those who know death also know that there are no appropriate words of consolation. There is no formula for what to say. There is only our presence and our support. There is little denying the difficulty of being there for one another in this way. Our natural tendency is like Pilate's. We would much rather ignore the situation.

One of our other concerns is whether or not there will be someone to hold and grieve for us when we die. Many persons fear they will be the one who is left behind . . . the last of the family bereft of friends. From time to time, most of us lack the confidence and positive self-image to feel assured that our life and death will make a difference to anyone. We enter life in the comforting arms of our mothers and yearn to have loving arms embrace us when we die.

Those who minister to the aged and terminally ill know better than most that the only insurance that we will die in someone's arms is our having lived in them. The ongoing relationships we have with one another are the foundation for our future. We die — in large measure — the way we live.

Throughout the world, the concern human persons have for one another and about their deaths have encouraged them to form support groups and relationships for those who are dying. More and more, we are becoming aware of our responsibility for the lives of all who form the human community.

Today we pray for those whose arms will hold the dead body of someone they love. We pray for the courage to do that in faith when one we love is gone. We pray for those who will hold us. Most of all, we pray for all those who will never have even the small consolation of that last moment.

Thoughts for Reflection

◀What are some of the occasions when the community has been called to "hold the dead" in their arms? because of relationship? because of responsibility?

◀Whom have you personally held to your breast in death?

◀What are your concerns about the persons who will be with you at the end of your life?

◀How have you experienced resurrection in the midst of death because of the presence of the community?

THE FOURTEENTH STATION
Jesus Is Placed in the Tomb

(courtesy of Anita Nicholas)

"They took the body of Jesus and bound it with burial cloths along with the spices, according to the Jewish burial custom. Now in the place where he had been crucified there was a garden, and in the garden a new tomb, in which no one had yet been buried."
(John 19:40-41)

Funeral and burial customs vary throughout the world. No matter what they might be, the ritual is for the sake of those who are left behind. The mourning ritual is intended to honor the dead, console the living, and to help all of us accept the reality of death. No matter what the religious or ethnic backgrounds, there are certain familiarities. While the Irish Catholic's formula for expressing sympathy is, "Sorry for your troubles," the Orthodox Jew greets those who mourn with the words: "May the Lord comfort you among the mourners of Zion and Jerusalem." Americans have no ethnic or religious formula to comfort others. Perhaps one will evolve to help individuals encompass the feelings beyond the words we say.

Similarly, the Kaddish prayer of the Jewish mourner is not a prayer about death. It glorifies God and prays for peace. The Mass of Christian Burial is not a ritual of despair but one of hope that glorifies the Lord and proclaims our faith in the establishment of the Kingdom. No matter what the form of ritual — the wake or the Jewish shivah, telling stories is central to the period of mourning. During this time, those who loved the deceased remember together. They tell the stories that are dear to them and a picture of the goodness of a human person is formed. This image forms the context for the resurrected person to be present once more — in a new way — with those she or he loved.

From time to time, I have wondered about the three days between Jesus' death and his resurrected appearance. As one examines the process of grief, we become aware that there is a time when we are unprepared for the depth of resurrection. We need the psychological and spiritual space for grieving before we can assimilate the joy of resurrection. We need to prepare ourselves for this new intensified presence.

I well remember the time following my father's death when we told those stories, when we clung to one another in the "wake ritual" and let the community comfort us. We were much like Jesus' followers in the upper room. We had to allow my father to "go so he could be with us" in a new way. What convinced us of his eternal life was not the absence of those days but the presence that followed as my family began once more to feel his influence. During that time, we forgot his overpowering physical presence and remembered his gentleness. We recalled the times when he forgave us and told stories about the events of our childhood that had been long forgotten. Today, I would have to say I feel his presence more profoundly than when he was physically with me.

Stories about death and burial are familiar to all of us. We tell them in a variety of ways dependent upon our culture and religious beliefs. We speak about interment chapels or graveside services. We go to the graves or we stay away. Underlying our practice is our belief that we will return to the ground from where we came.

"So there in the land of Moab, Moses, the servant of the Lord, died as the Lord had said, and he was buried in the ravine opposite Beth-peor in the land of Moab, but to this day no one knows the place of his burial." (Deuteronomy 34: 5-6)

Some of us know that we will never again lose a person who has meant as much as one we have already buried. Each wake reminds us of that loss. We grieve anew and we grieve still. We know, though, that we will in all likelihood bury others who have meant much to us. We, too, will finally turn to dust in a place not yet determined:

In a family cemetery plot.

In an unmarked grave in a foreign country.

In a grand tomb with an eternal flame.

In the walls of a mausoleum.

Today and tomorrow, throughout the world, thousands will be buried. We pray for them in a special way and we think, not without regret and not without hope, of the place where the body we have reverenced, the body that has been part of our person will one day turn to dust. We give praise and thanks to the Father who has sent Jesus to travel the way of the cross with us and lead us beyond the cross to resurrection.

There are many who would say there ought to be a fifteenth station remembering Jesus' resurrection. In fact, countless churches have incorporated such a station into their architecture. It is a valid and theologically sound practice. At the same time, each of us ought to be aware as we pray the stations of the cross that the underlying reality of each stop along the way — what continually gives us hope — is the faith we have in the resurrection. To consider the stations without this faith is to engage in a morbid re-enactment of death without life.

Life is filled with pain and suffering. No single event or series of events captures its fullness. Reflection on the passion of Jesus isolated from his total life and resurrection is a distortion. Jesus spent thirty-three years among us teaching us how to live. To reduce the reality of the incarnation and the reasons for it to only the passion, death, and resurrection is to diminish its importance.

Jesus walked the path toward death and resurrection every moment of his life just as we do. As we continually experience suffering in the midst of joy, he did too. The experience of pain was interwoven in the fullness of life. The moments of weeping were interspersed with laughter. He experienced the alienation of the community even while he was comforted by the love of those nearest him.

In many ways, the way of the cross is a ritual of all of life. It is a continuing reminder that life is not mere pleasure; nor is it only pain and agony.

As surely as Jesus came to bless our joys, he came to bless our sorrows. He came to tell us to live life and to love it. It is abundantly clear that those who do not value life will not look forward to "more life" — even in the form of resurrection.

Thoughts for Reflection

◀What comfort have you found in the rituals that surround death in your community?

◀Why is telling stories important during a time of grief?

◀What are some of the ways in which we can help those who mourn?

◀How does our experience of the grief prepare us for resurrection?

◀In what ways ought the stations of the cross be part of our total liturgical year rather than merely a Lenten reflection?

◀As you walk the way of the cross with the Lord, what are your feelings about the totality of Jesus' life? about the fullness of your own?